Monologue

Poems

by
Benn Sowerby

Order this book online at www.trafford.com
or email orders@trafford.com

Most Trafford titles are also available at major online book retailers.

Note for Librarians: A cataloguing record for this book is available from Library
and Archives Canada at www.collectionscanada.ca/amicus/index-e.html

Printed in Victoria, BC, Canada.

ISBN: 9781-4269-083-0-9

*Our mission is to efficiently provide the world's finest, most comprehensive
book publishing service, enabling every author to experience success.
To find out how to publish your book, your way, and have it available
worldwide, visit us online at www.trafford.com*

Trafford rev. 09/11/09

www.trafford.com

North America & international
toll-free: 1 888 232 4444 (USA & Canada)
phone: 250 383 6864 ♦ fax: 812 355 4082

Contents

Dies Irae.. 1

The Pool 3

The Encounter 5

Requiem.. 7

The Path 9

The Fall.. 11

Dew on the Leaf.. 13

A Scene Recalled 15

Wasted Moments 17

Evening.. 19

The Witness 21

The Secret 23

Autmn.. 25

Night Piece 27

Cornucopia 29

A Song of Sorrow 31

Woods in Autumn.. 33

True Intercourse 35

The Assailants 37

The Wind 39

A Fancy 41

Finis 43

Threnody 45

Misgiving 47

Monologue.. 49

The Empty Room 51

Retrospect 53

Recognition.. 57

Fulfilment 59

Re-awakening.. 61

Dies Irae

-

Beyond the parched grass blades starkly upthrust
Precipitately stirs a coil of dust,
A cypher enigmatical of all
That might in other circumstance befall.

Now even that is dead and time stands still
A crouching monster shadowed by the hill,
As if the world contracted in a thought
From boundless fancy to this less than nought.

The harsh sadistic impulse of the light
Beats on dust-powdered walls of glaring white,
And arid earth reiterates in vain
Its muffled rasping sigh of long-drawn pain.

So spreads the empty dawn with staring rays
Prohetic of inevitable days
When all is stilled but the last wild impotent curse
Throbbing throughout a tearless universe.

The Pool

-

In a lost country
Silvered with moonlight
Where the heart sickens
For unknown things

We have wandered onward
To a tarn in the mountains
Where the soft rain drops
Seldom dip.

The sand there is strangely
Scored with faint farings
And the water glimmers
Darkly above.

I know not, and often
I wonder dimly
What could attract us
To that far pool.

Silence and darkness
Encircle those mountains.
Solitude friendless
Girdles the waste.

Yet in the hollow
Of that small basin
Lies a forgotten
Image we knew.

Lost in the shadow,
Vainly we search for it.
Mocking us ever
The surface reflects,

Like a broken mirror,
Unnumbered fragments
In hues irridescent
But guessed at in gloom.

The Encounter

-

"Far have I journeyed. Rough the way
With cheerless solitude for guide.
And still before me dims the day,
And still behind glooms dark night-tide.

Alone, with hope a slender beam,
I know not where these steps may tend,
Which but for you wind out in dream,
Nor what may be the journey's end.

Have you no words to lure me on?
What comfort for the stranger lies,
A reflex where bright hopes have shone,
Within those dark untroubled eyes?"

"I too a stranger wander here
Seeking an unkown distant bourne,
A child of sorrow, my lamp a tear,
Ere yet my heart had learned to mourn."

Requiem

-

Though they are all gone
And the dust lies lightly over them
But deep, deeper than the graves of men,
Perhaps in some far grove, where the moon shone
In ancient days with silver splendour, still
A late bird fluting low may sadly fill
The brooding silences, as many then,
Singing in solitude their last high requiem.

So the dusk-haunted ways
With a dim memory even yet
May echo to the cold stars faintingly
To prove through indistinguishable nights and days
They are not lost, till silence heap once more
The tufted weed about the half-closed door
And only through sleep's hushed eternity
Thin phantom voices hesitantly fret.

The Path

-

None comes here now,
Where of old
A track was beaten through the underbrush,
Only down the long avenue
Of beeches topped with gold
While the deep hush
Of evening fills the wood
The shadows brood
And, as I wait
Leaning here upon the weathered gate,
Deepen to universal gloom.
And still I stand
Until my thoughts
Merge in the shadows and
Wander away in the dusk.
Perhaps I shall never know
Why I wait thus,
Listening, watching,
Wondering will it continue so.
For now it seems,
So long I have waited in vain,
Nothing will ever happen
Until in dreams,
Seeking fulfilment of unknown desire,
I sink to peace again.

The Fall
-
Once sunlight dappled the garden
  From a calm, vacant sky,
And time with promise laden
  Slid silent by.

But the tree awoke from sleeping.
  Eve trembled beneath its leaves
With a light heart turned to weeping
  For the hope that deceives.

Sunset, a molten river,
  Flowed over the tree unseen
And the swift form lost in a quiver
  Of gold and green.

A wind mourned in the garden.
  The crisping leaves swept by.
Autumn was born in Eden
  Of a tear and a sigh.

Dew on the Leaf

-

Within this globe of water lies
A reflex of unending skies,
A universe, minutely traced,
Of clearest blue with white enchased.
Strange that so vast a tract should be
Enclosed here thus so accurately!
So still and distant, yet so near
It seems, within this crystal sphere,
One almost fancies one has caught
The wings of time in swifter thought,
And sips eternity in brief
Inconsequence until the leaf
Where rests the mirror trembles and
That little world's a vanished land,
And time, as suddenly released,
Wheels on as it had never ceased.

A Scene Recalled

-

Here is the path.
Flowers still ramble here.
I have seen them blooming so
Many a year
Far and near
Through the woods. In Autumn months
The rain spills through the trees
Dripping and spattering softly,
And one sees
The sodden still drinking.
Here thrushes too
Rejoice yet in the rain
Just as they used to do
So many years ago.
But only the bent trees can know
Which fall of leaves marked that untroubled time
Which I recall now in my careless rhyme.
So distant seems that hour
That now its pain
Is melancholy-sweet
And even a thought to dwell upon,
So that as one
Who lifts a piece of china plate
Weighing its fragmentary beauty
In the mind,
Lets his thoughts wander in pretty fantasy
And half-limns a tale
That might have been;
So I
Paint in my thought a delicate history,
But part-imagined: thus
I view the scene
As on a painted tile,
Unmoved,
And with appreciative smile
Turn from its pleasant half-conned mystery
Back to reality.

Wasted Moments

-

The subtle moments, sliding on,
Like threaded beads link one to one
A slender chain: then all are gone.

All perfect in variety
Of amber, coral, ivory
We let them fall unendingly.

Like children fascinated still
Lightly we toy at fancy's will
With each, uncomprehending, till

Another gleams ere that is cast,
Attracts our gaze, and then as fast
It too is dropped into the past:

And, careless in our old infancy
What vast eternity may lie
Between quick thought and thought, we die.

Evening
-
A grey light falls on the downs,
And the light leaves falling
Whisper, as the wind moans,
Calling,
In music voiceless to the one who hears
From the bare hill-side,
Of countless years
That have mounded deep
Leaf-mould beneath the trees.
No sound
Wakes on the stillness an echo of life:
But as in the gap,
Where the cart track winds
To the heart of the wood,
The dull light peers
With a fuller ray
To its secret deep
Where sleep
Broods silent, veiling
Its mystery:
So a darker day
Once lit the scene
Of a well-known way,
With a new half-light disclosing
Unguessed-at beauty.
And so indeed it has ever been
That grief may serve
For a clearer vision
Unveiling truth from its secrecy.
Should I then complain
Of the sultry day,
Of scentless rain,
Or of friendless weather?-
When the lovliest form
That life can borrow
Is born from the silent heart
Of sorrow.

The Witness

-

Dead tales dream here forgotten
Among these mouldering walls.
Yet though the towers are rotten
An unknown voice still calls,
Echoing through their silence
    When the dim night-tide falls.

And faint bells then ring clearly
In tones softer than of old,
Their chimes still sounding cheerly
Over the distant wold,
Though none can now unravel
    The tales they might have told.

Dead hearts may lie unfriended,
Lost hopes be buried deep:
What though their dreams are ended!
None can for ever weep.
And death will prove his bounty
    In stores unknown to sleep.

When weeds have won the towers,
And the tall spires decayed,
The walls yielded to flowers
In crumbled dust arrayed,
Nought will remain to witness
    The ruin time has made.

But still the wind soft-calling
Will lisp on the still air,
With fable death forestalling,
Nor cheating unaware,
And so sing on their burden
    Till time too sleep ensnare.

The Secret

-

The night catches its breath
In a dreamless quiet, and still
Is the heron's call: not death
But sleep alone breathes in the chill.

The stars glimmer remote,
Unguaged by the thoughts of men,
Names only learned by rote,
Disclosing nought to their ken.

Yet in the day's full light
A mystery too remains,
For something hidden from sight
Ever a secret retains.

Never the river's flow
Tells aught that its pebbles can hear,
And the reed can never know
What the wind whispers in its ear.

Autmn

-

As the wind whistles through the cracks of the old
barn
The crazy door flaps open with a sigh,
And then swings creaking back on rusty hinges.
On days like this the wind buffets the trees
This way and that in wild and careless play.
It strows the chill, bleak yard with wisps of straw;
And from the gate where it piled the russet leaves
It blows them scurrying to the edge of the pond,
Where the water wakes in long grey curving ripples,
To set them flying back suddenly, fast as
The billowy clouds which throng the cheerless sky. -
And yet I marked not Summer passing by.

Night Piece

-

Softly and sadly
Lapping low banks the rippling wavelets of the river
Croon as they leap.

Slowly and sadly
Shaking its silver-burdened locks the willow
Bows to the moon.

Strangely and sadly
The cry of a night bird in the distant hollow
Echoes again.

Softly and sadly
Will not night's beauty tremble thus for ever
Above my sleep!

Cornucopia

-

Placed here upon the terrace, where the view
Recedes in mirage of a mist-grey hue,
Spilling profusely its full burden down
Over the stone steps etched in green and brown,
We fancy it is poured for our delight
With rich fruits ripened in a glowing light.

Such fruits as these I have never seen before,
Save in imagined orchards whose bright store,
Smoothed by the soft caress of star-crowned night,
Hangs in full clusters barred with amber light,
Or, half embedded in a mesh of leaves,
Allures the eye to each russet point that cleaves
The deep-set verdure. Round each rugged bole,
Knee-deep in grass, where round-bellied apples roll
Spurned in their dance, rough satyrs frisk and leap:
While goat-foot Pan encourages to sleep
With his wild notes that cheer the dance along
    The over-drowsed Silenus.

                So the throng
Capers, unheeding all but the gay round,
Weaving fantastic shadows on the ground,
Till suddenly the mischievous god espies
A band of nymphs, and eager for his prize
Throws down his pipe. The satyrs follow after
Urging on haste with sounds of uncouth laughter.
Silenus wakes, and rubs his eyes, looks round,
And, heavily rising, at a lumbering bound
Eagerly ambles off in drunken gait,
Desire outspeeding his more piteous state.
So all are gone. Pan's pipe alone, that fell
There on the beaten grass, remains to tell
Of the giddy rout.

        And on the terrace here,
All fancy fled, the clinging mist sweeps near,
And these stone fruits and garlands but remain
To mock regrets through a thin veil of rain.

29

A Song of Sorrow

Steep, steep is the hill-side,
And as we climb
We cannot distinguish
The beat of time.

Deep, deep are the waters
Of the fathomless sea
Where we yet can fancy
The light is free.

Sleep, sleep is the burden
Of all our song
Of the twisted days
That bear us along.

Weep. weep for the passing
Of this cold clay,
For none can lighten
The secret way.

Woods in Autumn

-

Here the rains of Autum swell
Leaf-mould deep on earth.The birds
Hop from branch to branch and tell
Secrets never born in words.
Here with muffled footsteps stray
When the evening air is still,
When the sun with slanting ray
Topples over yonder hill.
Treading softly, you will hear,
Mournful in autumnal strains
Hidden from the noon-dulled ear,
Muted notes and sad refrains.
Here the brambles straggle wide:
Over path and mossy bank
Bluebells linger, sapless, dried:
Faintly rustling rank on rank
Dead wood sanicle yet sways.
Sodden leafage underfoot
Almost audibly decays.
Every voice now, sad or mute,
Strangely hints of withered life.
Autumn's glory fading so
Leaves the brambles only rife,
All else rotting, drooping low.
Yet a spirit wanders here,
Threading in and out the trees,
Through late leafage thin and sere,
And she has no part with these.
Hers the mounting sap within
Silently, invisibly,
Proving earth's unfailing kin.
Hers the murmur, clear and free,
Of the yet unfrozen brook:
Hers that sudden trembling note
Where the dark top twigs just shook:
And maybe she has for coat
The last rich glow above the hill
That seems to warm the shrinking air.
So she drifts through Autumn's chill
Haunting her unbounded lair
Shadowy, unwatched.But when
Life awakes with Spring's green birth
She will prove her care again,
Beating in the breast of earth.

True Intercourse

-

If heart to heart can ear and ear deceive
These subtle intonations now grown stale
Cannot explicitly relieve
The thought's full complement but fail
In overtuning innuendo thus
To analyse the still essential <u>us</u>.
Break now the glittering thread and throw aside
The ineffective limits of the past;
Lay bare the occasion: shew where sprit lied
In fault of right expression, and at last
Denuded, hunted from our snug retreats
We stand revealed beyond the old deceits.

The Assailants

-

Silent they stood and eyed each other, two
Who in a younger world had laughed at life
And sipped its beauty till they dreamed anew
Of happier days that held no hint of strife.
Dull sunken eyes, remorseless now, peered out
From hollow faces; where perhaps had shone
A fierce appeal, now only gleamed a doubt,
Mistrustful questioning. As they still gazed on
Deep shadows fell about them, hemmed them in.
Caged by their own desires they mutely stared.
Dumb thoughts reflected from souls hid within
Reached not deaf ears. So for a time they shared
The pregnant minutes. Then in silence turned
And parted in secret sorrow undiscerned.

The Wind

-

So the day passes in cloud and mist and rain,
And the wind gathers into a sigh complaining.

Here on the downs the wind seems often old
And sad, weary even of Spring's unfolding.

Many a day I paced the downs alone
Long ago, lightly all cares disowning.

Sometimes the wind would bend me to its will:
Yet even so I could feel in its strength life thrilling,

And joy in its mastery as I strode along
Beneath a sky fantastic with white clouds
thronging.

Now it seems old; yet I know it will not be so
Always, though for me it is fruitless knowing.

The wind will recapture its spirit, I never again,
Seeking but earth now fragrant with fitful raining.

A Fancy

-

A dead leaf swings to the ground
Slowly curvetting,
Its little whisper drowned
By the rain's light fretting

As the dead leaf of desire
Spent faintly flutters
In the cool rain that a shyer
Silence utters.

Finis

When all is ended,
     The last tale told,
The last weed withered,
     The last heart cold,
And dream proves twilight
     Grey and old:

When the sea has scattered
     Its last light spray
And in voiceless music
     Sinks away,
All earth's mouths muted
     Save still decay:

What wind of Eden
     On the quiet air
Will stir that dust
     From its ancient lair
To a silence deeper
     Than thought may share?

Threnody

-

The tall trees that once again are shedding
Their withered leafage on the steep hill-side
Stand as of old fantastically spreading
Their baring branches interweaving wide.

And here long ago as I remember
You stood to view the landscape stretching bleak
While the lorn wind of late September
Blew dark strands of hair across your cheek.

A low sky cast long shadows in the valley
Over grey roof and street and spire
Till, as we gazed, with swift and sudden sally
Twilight extinguished the last faint glowing fire

Over the western hills. Then quickly turning
You hid your face in delicate cupped hand
As though some vaster image there discerning,
And murmured words I could not understand:

Now years have passed between us, and their meaning
Is shadowed forth in grief and dull despair
And these tall trees which yesterday were greening
Wake empty echoes of the young and fair.

Misgiving

-

Are not the features fairly moulded, beautiful
    The graceful curves of cheek and lip and ear?
When I see these so delicate petal-cool
    I know all longing consummated here.

Yet when I look within those deep cave-haunted eyes
    And see the furtive shadows fleeting there,
Almost I cede a truth my faith denies
    And grapple vainly with my own despair.

Monologue
-

Then a faint murmur through the night rises to tell you
    that the wind sleeps not though now the waters are still
    and a spell is cast over the ocean deepening the silence
    while the stars are hidden in mystery and the air thrills
    to an unknown voice that is pleading in soft veiled accents
    for you know not what, your heart refusing to listen;
    know that Earth is my parent, and loves me, and will not be silent
    because sleep is alone now, rocking the cradle of care.

But when at last comes a night that is pillowed in silence
    and the great pines shudder and tremble and then are still,
    when only a breeze scarce audible, winging so softly,
    sings in your saddened heart the refrain of lost years
    till it faints in the darkness of sleep and becomes, unbidden,
    one with your thoughts which flow in an endless stream;
    you may know then that Earth has grown cold for the death of a lover,
    ere you turn to forget in the joyless peace of your dreams.

The Empty Room

-

It is so long now since I swept this room for you,
Turned out everything, even table and chair.
The windows smile no longer as they used to do.
The pictures are gone, leaving the four walls bare.
It was your wish: and gladly I made room for you.

I see now I was wrong in giving way to you.
Old comforts and associations gone,
Dancing upon the bare boards seems so gay to you
You will not furnish it again. - Again alone,
I wonder regretfully why I make way for you.

Retrospect

-

Since then we are parting
and the choice has been made
I would not be importunate but enter unafraid
the gloomy vista that I now exchange
for light-linked hours falling without change.
Yet for a moment let me take you back with me
through the smooth sweet days of a simple
immortality.
Spring shall renew in you an eager expectancy.

Bright bird eyes glancing down lit avenues
saw a shadow quiver through the young green leaves
innocent of treachery when the net retrieves
sharp sunlight splintered in irridescent hues.
Here is no anachronism but neglected birthright,
green of the woodland, gold of the sun,
days ripe and fragrant, burnished and apple bright
declining to the blossom now their light is done.

Day breaks quietly over those lost latitudes
with hesitant thin piping of half-awakened birds,
feigned indecision that animates illusion:
so the scene is set and life enters from the wings.
And so may you sail again the frail craft of fancy
on that wind-rippled sea of fragrant pink and white.
This is our triumph reentering the garden
Time has no power to banish us again:
He is a stranger in our recreated Eden,
for us, though not for him, the sword flames in vain.

A new dawn shall light us straying in the meadows
where the larks rise singing from the dew-pointed
blades
and the mist withdrawing over the low hedgerows
shews the giant earth netted in light silken threads.
But these cannot hold him when the silver horn
echoes through the copses for a new day born.
Earth wakes slowly from dreams of deeper memory,
the old giant stirs and murmurs in his sleep.

So we seek our emblems through wind-rippled
gossamer,
a silver ocean of inconstant tides,
our trophies the soft red tassel of the hazel blossom

and primroses starring the mossed woodland rides.

Shall we then be bound to a season of transition,
snare the young sun and arrest the mounting sap?
The eyes would weary of a constant expectancy,
promise unfulfilled would sink to inanition.

So our year revolves, our sun is at its zenith,
and again we wander in the tall arched woods
down cool-leaved cloisters dapple-lit with sunlight
filtered through their tracery. The long day broods
sullen and indolent, and we too are caught
squandering our leisure by the old canal
in a drowsy listlessness that clogs all thought.
Time is an anomaly but the slow hours slide
bringing us release untempered by regret,
for now we pick the richest threads to weave into our
tapestry
gladly remembering that our sun must set.

Summer's greenery is fired to gleaming bronze,
the trees' bright armouries glitter with its gold,
and the ways are carpeted with russet embroidery.
Here are worthy emblems for memory to hold.
So let us seek again the ripe fruits of autumn,
apple and quince, walnut and pear.
This shall be our chosen season, the season of
fulfilment,
these the buried tokens that recall us there.

But lest these memories should haunt us with
nostalgia
we will strip the branches, leave the landscape bare,
the trees, gaunt cyphers, stencilling their traceries
on the still curtain of the cold grey air.
Earth congealed wakes in muffled silence
to a copper sun glowing in an empty sky.
Wheeling high above the stagnant ploughland
a windy cloud of rooks goes straggling by.
So the scene grows dark, illusion vanishes.
In silence we turn to what new destiny?

Recognition

-

Now that you are gone from me I feel
The sure insistence of your love that sets
Sunward at morning when the mists reveal
Earth's beauty naked through their silver nets:

And I would climb with you toward the dawn,
Beyond the heavy-scented bloom of night,
A gleaming arrow of the huntress drawn
Straight and strong from the bow to hazardous flight.

So in the purer spaces unconfined,
Our course directed ever to the light,
We shall not fear the brightness that can blind.
We shall have gained a rarer thing than sight.

Fulfilment

-

Stand where you stood, so,
On the sleek hill-side,
And the waves chuckled softly below
And the far gulls cried.
Still the same note, wistful and faint, is borne
Over the sunset path where the waves mourn.

Now for the last time
We stand here alone
As when, till the sparlking rime
Enspangling your hair shone
With an unearthly brilliance, we have stood before
So many times. Now it must be no more.

So it is that I cast
A last long look
Over your form, and the past
Wells as from hope forsook,
That, though in forgetfulness memory return, even
yet
In the remembering I may forget.

Look no more behind
After this hour.
To all but the future be blind.
So have we power
To cast aside all trivial desire
And light new love at old love's funeral pyre.

Re-awakening

-

Since all these friends have passed and you alone
Have paused to wonder if the hidden past
Could utter one small grace-note of the truth
I look on you as one whom I have known
From childhood's spring and see the sands upcast
Which flowed so swiftly over our missed youth.

Look in these eyes now! Do you see some spark
Of that lost fire which burned in other times?
Perhaps even these two mirrors are burnt out
And will not serve for witness in the dark
That glooms about my universe and climbs
To cloud high heaven in a final doubt.

Draw closer then. I will not let you go
Till I have shewn you where the end must be.
So lip to lip we grow insensate here
Of all but that one truth they would not know,
Those friends who passed unheeding. We shall see
Still dawn of life strike blind the eyes of fear.